Visiting the Doctor

By
Joanna Brundle

BookLife

©2017
Book Life
King's Lynn
Norfolk PE30 4LS

ISBN: 978-1-78637-070-9

A catalogue record for this book
is available from the British Library.

Written by:
Joanna Brundle

Edited by:
Grace Jones

Designed by:
Danielle Jones

Contents

What is a Doctor?

Friendly Doctor

Big Smile

Doctors are friendly people who look after us when we are poorly.

They tell us what is wrong and help us to get better.

Why do we Visit the Doctor?

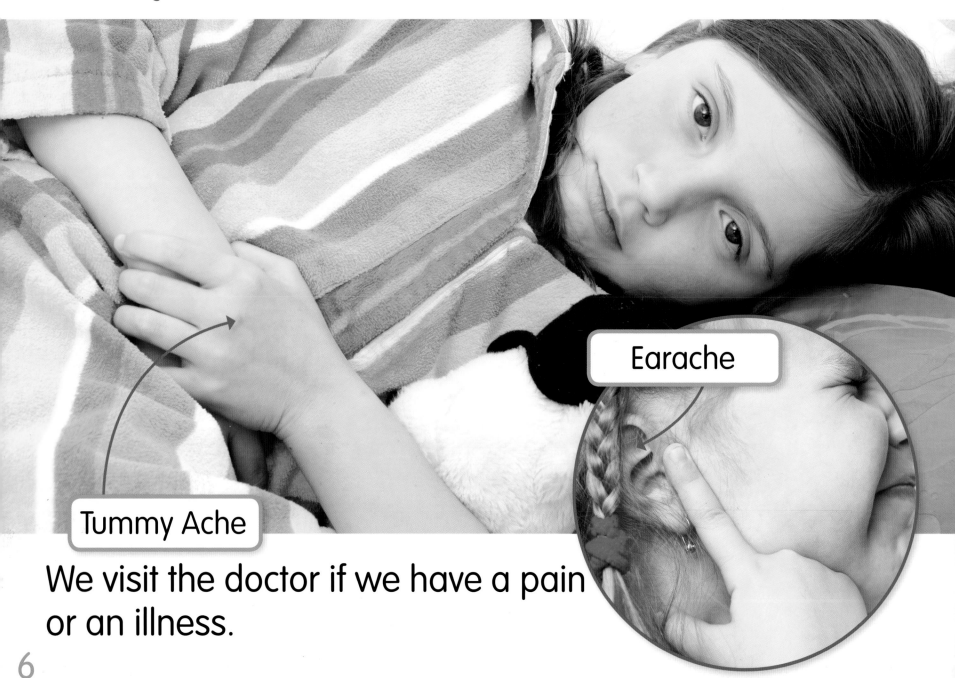

Earache

Tummy Ache

We visit the doctor if we have a pain or an illness.

6

We visit the doctor if we have an accident or need an injection.

Injection

Cut Leg

In the Waiting Room

We check-in here.

We tell the person at the desk we have arrived so the doctor knows we are there.

We sit in the waiting room until the doctor is ready to see us.

Waiting Room

Chairs

Desk

9

What Does the Doctor Look Like?

Dress

Doctor

Desk

Mummy

White Coat

Doctor

The doctor usually wears ordinary clothes but sometimes wears a white coat.

When doctors check us, they wear gloves and, sometimes, a mask.

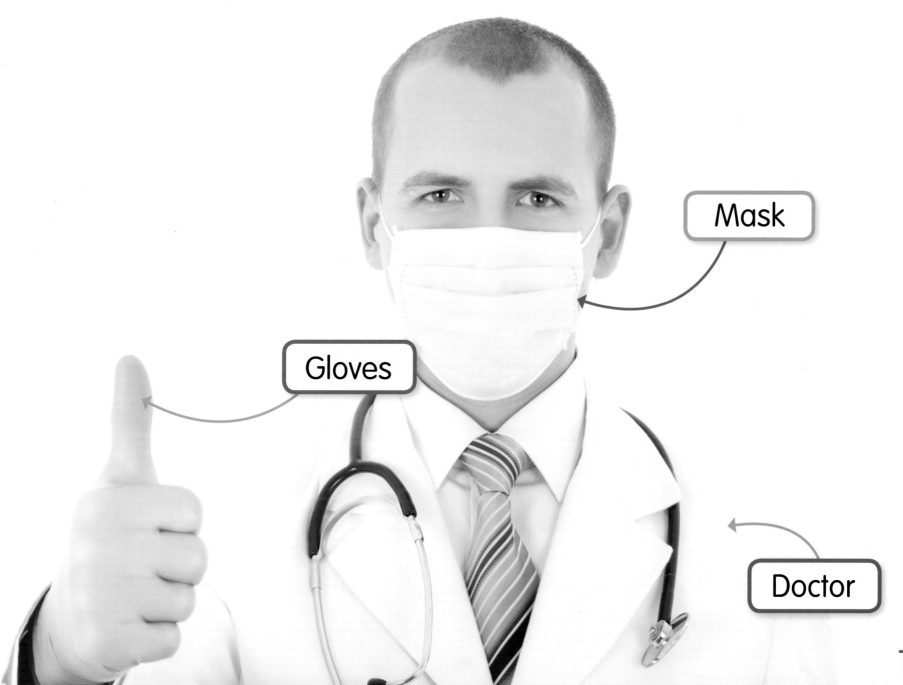

Mask

Gloves

Doctor

Inside the Doctor's Room

Doctor

Telephone

Mummy

Desk

The doctor sits at a desk. We can sit on Mummy's lap.

The doctor washes his or her hands, then checks us.

Sink

Bed

Doctor

What Does the Doctor Do?

Stethoscope

Doctor

Teddy

Say "aaah!"

Spatula

The doctor listens to our chest and tummy with a stethoscope.

The doctor checks our temperature.
Illness can make us very hot.

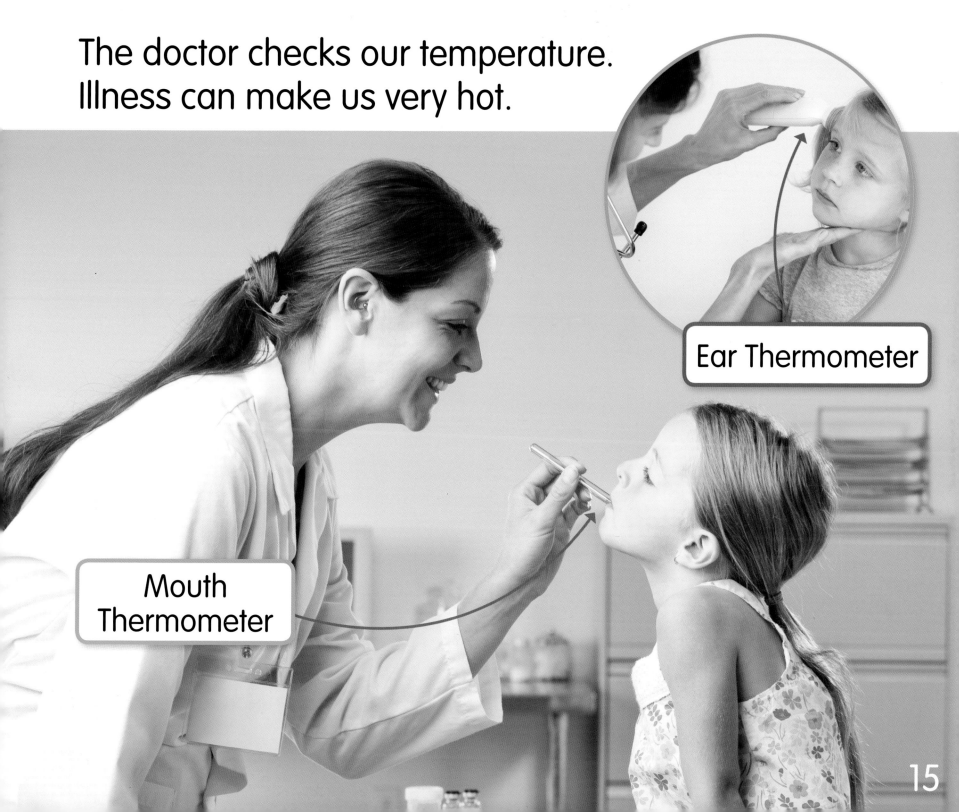

Ear Thermometer

Mouth
Thermometer

15

I Spy ...

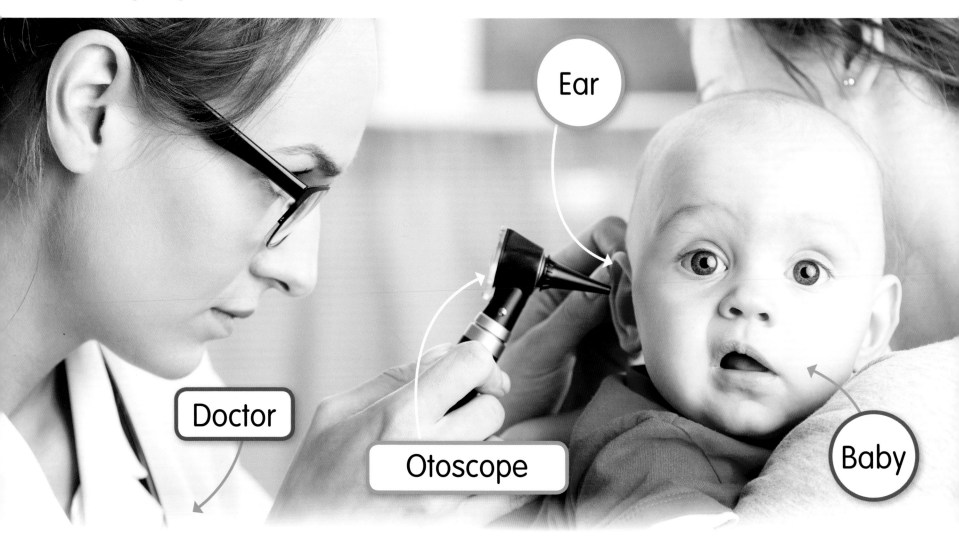

The doctor uses an otoscope to look in our ears.

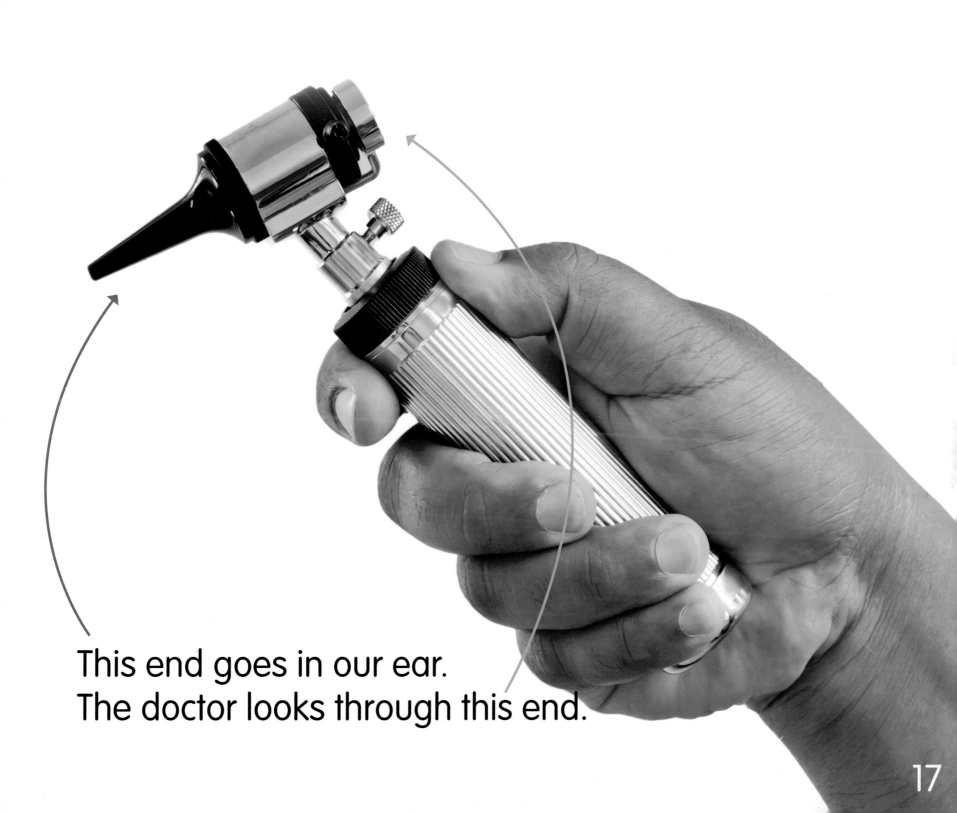

This end goes in our ear.
The doctor looks through this end.

The Nurse

Nurse

Some illnesses mean we have to be checked often by the nurse.

The nurse helps us to take our medication properly and to stay healthy.

Inhaler

It doesn't hurt!

Let's get our Medicine

Mummy

Doctor

Prescription

The doctor writes which medicine we need on a prescription.

We take it to the pharmacy. The pharmacist gives us our medicine.

Mummy

Medicines

Going Home

We make another appointment if the doctor needs to see us again.

High five! We're better!

We rest and take our medicine.
Soon, we feel better!

Plastic Spoon

Medicine

23

Index

Photo Credits

Abbreviations: l-left, r-right, b-bottom, t-top, c-centre, m-middle.

Front Cover l – Monkey Business Images. Front Cover ml – wavebreakmedia. Front Cover mr – Oksana Kuzmina. Front Cover r – Andresr. 1 – AJP. 2 – Pressmaster. 3 – Luis Molinero. 4 – Ilike. 5 – Darren Baker. 5r - Rob Hainer. 6inset - Anna Omelchenko. 6 - PHILIPIMAGE 6inset– Gladskikh Tatiana. 7 - 2xSamara.com. 8 - Monkey Business Images. 9 – Tyler Olson. 10 – Monkey Business Images. 11 – Di Studio. 12 – Monkey Business Images. 13 – PhotoSerg. 14 – Alexander Raths. 15 – AVAVA. 16 – Photographee.eu. 17 – oumjeab. 18 – adriaticfoto. 19 – Levent Konuk. 20 – Photographee.eu. 21 – Tyler Olson 21inset – Dmitry Kalinovsky. 22 – emilie zhang. 23 – wavebreakmedia 23inset – VGstockstudio. Images are courtesy of Shutterstock.com. With thanks to Getty Images, Thinkstock Photo and iStockphoto.